Sports Stars

REGGIE JACKSON

From Superstar to Candy Bar

By George Vass

 CHILDRENS PRESS, CHICAGO

Cover photograph: Richard Pilling
Inside photographs courtesy of United Press International, pages 6, 9, 14, 20, 27, 32, 34, 36, 40, and 44; and Carl Skalak, Jr./ Opticom, page 18.

ABOUT THE AUTHOR

George Vass, for twenty years a sportswriter with the *Chicago Daily News*, has followed major league baseball for most of his career in journalism. He covered the Chicago Cubs and Chicago White Sox on a regular beat basis for *The Daily News*.

In addition, Vass has written half a dozen books on sports subjects. Among them are *George Halas and the Chicago Bears, The Chicago Black Hawks Story*, and *Champions of Sports: Adventures in Courage*. Vass is a regular contributor to several publications, including *Baseball Digest* and *Hockey Digest* magazines.

Library of Congress Cataloging in Publication Data

Vass, George.
  Reggie Jackson: from superstar to candy bar.

  (Sports stars)
  SUMMARY: A biography of the Yankee batter who broke
Babe Ruth's record by hitting three home runs in a row
in the 1977 World Series.
    1. Jackson, Reggie—Juvenile literature. 2. Base-
ball players—United States—Biography—Juvenile litera-
ture. [1. Jackson, Reggie. 2. Baseball players.
3. Afro-Americans—Biography] I. Title. II. Series.
GV865.J32V37   796.357'092'4 [B] [92]   78-21511
ISBN 0-516-04303-X

  2 3 4 5 6 7 8 9 10 11 12 R 85 84 83 82 81 80 79

Sports Stars

REGGIE JACKSON

From Superstar to Candy Bar

"Reggie! Reggie! Reggie!" Every one of the 60,000 fans in Yankee Stadium was screaming for Reggie Jackson.

It was game six of the 1977 World Series. Reggie was at bat for the New York Yankees. Pitching for the Los Angeles Dodgers was Charlie Hough.

The Yankees had won three of the first five games. If they won this game they would be the champions. The Yankees were leading 7-3 in the eighth inning. Reggie came to bat for the fourth time in the game. He had already hit two home runs.

Reggie waited for Hough's first pitch. Hough threw a knuckleball, a slow pitch that floats to the plate. It is hard to hit. But Reggie sent the ball flying with a tremendous swing. It soared 450 feet into center field.

"Reggie! Reggie! Reggie!" the fans screamed, jumping to their feet. Reggie ran around the bases, tipping his cap to the crowd.

He was thinking, "Hey man, wow, that's three."

Reggie could not believe it. In a Series game he had hit three home runs in a row. No one ever had done that before. Babe Ruth once hit three home runs in a Series game, but not in a row. Reggie had broken Babe Ruth's record.

The Yankees won the game, 8-4, and the Series. They were the world champions. At the final out, Reggie raced toward the dugout from right field. He desperately dodged the crowd. Thousands of fans ran onto the field. They wanted to touch him, to pat him on the back.

In the noisy, jammed Yankee locker room, Reggie was surrounded by reporters. They all wanted

to know how Reggie felt before he hit his third home run. "At that point I couldn't lose," Reggie said. "Not after hitting the first two. All I had to do was show up at the plate. The fans were going to cheer me even if I struck out. So the last one was strictly dreamland."

The entire game was "dreamland" for Reggie. His first time at bat he walked. The next three times up he hit the first pitch for a home run. In the fifth game Reggie had also hit a home run his last time up. So now he held the record for hitting four home runs in a row.

Reggie was voted the Most Valuable Player of the World Series. He led all hitters with a .450 batting average. He hit a record five home runs in six games.

Reporters and fans now compared Reggie with two former great Yankee players, Babe Ruth and

Joe DiMaggio. "I'm not Joe DiMaggio," Reggie said. "I'm not Babe Ruth. Those two guys were great, great baseball players. I'm a good baseball player. I don't know if I'm a great one."

If Reggie does not think himself a great player, it is not because he is always modest. He is very outspoken. He says what he thinks. He believes it is important to be honest. He has deep feelings about some things. He is a religious man. He never forgets that he is black. He believes that many blacks do not get the chances he has had.

During the World Series Reggie had a little picture of Jackie Robinson on his uniform belt. Jackie Robinson was the first black allowed to play major league baseball. "I dedicated this season to him," Reggie said. "Do you think he's proud of me?"

In 1947 when Robinson played his first game for the Brooklyn Dodgers, Reggie was just a baby. Reginald Martinez Jackson was born in Pennsylvania. He grew up in Cheltenham, a suburb of Philadelphia. There were few blacks in town, but the young Reggie did not suffer from racial prejudice. Still, he never forgot that he was born black and that his family was very poor.

When asked about his boyhood, Reggie said, "I would like some kid to read the Reggie Jackson story and say, 'I haven't had anything to eat for the last four days, but I am going to be able to make it. . . . I am going to be like Reggie Jackson in believing that God will get me through this and that I am going to try to do the right things at the right time.' "

Reggie was the second youngest of six children. When Reggie was six, his parents were divorced.

His mother and three of the children moved to Maryland. Reggie, his older brother Joe, and his sister Beverly stayed with their father.

Martinez Jackson was a tailor. While Reggie grew up, his father delivered dry-cleaning. Later he opened a tailor shop. Mr. Jackson left for work early. Reggie had to get ready for school by himself. Sometimes there was nothing for breakfast. He would go to school hungry. Sometimes he wouldn't eat dinner until his father came home late at night.

Reggie's father worked hard. He never earned much money. Somehow he managed. "He did what he had to do to get by," Reggie said. "He got his kids fed, clothed, and grown up."

Mr. Jackson was very strict. He expected Reggie to do what he was told and never to complain.

Reggie gives a piggy-back ride to a young admirer.

If Reggie asked for money, Mr. Jackson would ask, "What have you done to earn it?" He made Reggie help him on the delivery truck and then gave him a dime or a quarter. He expected Reggie to work and do his best. "Always go at things hard," Mr. Jackson said. If Reggie tried to make an excuse, his father said, "I don't want to hear any 'ar ray boo.' " That was his way of saying that he did not want Reggie to give him any baloney.

As a young man Mr. Jackson was a boxer and a semi-pro baseball player. When Reggie was seven his father taught him to play softball.

Reggie was good. At Cheltenham High School Reggie starred in baseball, football, and track. In baseball, he played the outfield because he had a strong arm and could throw very hard. He ran fast. He was the best hitter on the team. In track, he was a sprinter and high jumper. In football, he was a running back and averaged eight yards a carry.

Reggie loved sports, and he was a very good student. But he liked sports best because he was so good that people noticed him. He wanted to be liked and admired. It made him feel good when he was praised for hitting a home run or scoring a touchdown. Maybe that was because there was no one to praise him at home.

Reggie wanted to be a better athlete. He listened carefully to Chuck Mehelich, his baseball coach. He always took extra batting practice.

Once Reggie was hurt because he practiced batting until it was too dark to see well. Reggie asked for high inside fast balls. The pitcher threw wild. Reggie lost sight of the ball. It hit him on the jaw. He fell to the ground, his face covered with blood.

Reggie was rushed to the hospital. His jaw was broken in three places. The doctors wired his jaw. But three days later Reggie took out the wires himself, because they bothered him. Soon he was playing baseball again. At bat, he dug in as firmly as before, with no sign of fear.

When Reggie was seventeen, his father left Cheltenham. He did not return for six months. Reggie became angry and quiet. "I was lonely," Reggie said. "I was sad all the time . . . until he got back. It's a bad memory for me."

While his father was gone, Reggie got into trouble. He was in a gang that picked fights. He talked back to his teachers. He was suspended from school three times.

He took out his anger on the football field. In a game a player hit him in the mouth. One of his teeth broke. Reggie wanted to get even. He told

his quarterback, "Let's run that play again." Reggie took the football. He ran directly at the player who had hit him. The player had already been knocked down, but Reggie viciously ran over him anyway.

Mr. Jackson came home during Reggie's senior year. Reggie calmed down. He began to think about what he wanted to do. He was good at football and at baseball. As a senior he batted .550. Many of his hits were home runs. When he didn't play right field, he pitched. He pitched three no-hit, no-run games.

Several major league scouts wanted Reggie to play baseball. Many colleges offered him a football scholarship.

Reggie's father told him to go to college. He could get an education and play sports, too. They

The first batting practice of spring training in Fort Lauderdale, Florida, 1977.

chose Arizona State University at Tempe. The school, A.S.U., was known for its fine baseball teams. Reggie could play both baseball and football.

Reggie played freshman football on the Sun Devils. He averaged seven yards a carry until he hurt his knee. He missed several games. When he returned, the coaches made him a defensive back. Reggie did not like that. "The offense is fun, not the defense," he said. "I like to have fun."

In spring Reggie made the baseball team. The coach was Bobby Winkles, who later became a major league manager. Winkles was very impressed with Reggie's batting. Reggie was one of the few players who could hit a curve ball almost as well as a fast ball.

Reggie was big. He was six feet tall and weighed 200 pounds. He could hit the ball hard and far left-handed. But Reggie had a weakness. If the pitcher threw a slow ball, a "change-up," when Reggie was expecting a fast ball, he would overswing and miss it. Winkles worked to correct this fault. "Don't lunge at the ball," Winkles told Reggie. "Wait until you see the ball leave the pitcher's hand. You'll be able to time it better." Winkles also helped Reggie improve his fielding. He had trouble catching fly balls. Winkles made Reggie chase fly balls until his legs were sore.

In his sophomore year Reggie became the Sun Devils' center fielder. He was the "clean up" hitter, batting fourth in the lineup. He quickly became one of the best college players in America. He batted .327 in 52 games, getting 66 hits in 202 times at bat. He hit 15 home runs and drove in 65 runs. He stole 15 bases. In one game he hit two home runs, two doubles, and a triple, and drove in seven runs.

The Kansas City Athletics sent scout Bob Zuk to watch Reggie play. Zuk told the A's owner, Charles O. Finley, "Reggie is a very good baseball prospect. He is a sure-fire major leaguer. He can become a star." The A's took Reggie first in the free agent draft. In June, 1966, Reggie accepted a $95,000 bonus from the A's and quit college.

The A's sent Reggie to play for one of their minor league teams, at Lewiston, Maine. Reggie did so well in 12 games there that the A's sent him to their other minor league team, at Modesto, California. In 56 games at Modesto, Reggie batted .299, with 21 home runs.

The next season the A's sent Reggie to their top minor league team at Birmingham, Alabama. He batted .293 in 114 games, with 17 home runs and 58 runs batted in. He was chosen the Southern League Player of the Year. He was so good that the A's called him up to Kansas City to finish the 1967 season with them. At 21, Reggie was a major leaguer.

During spring training of 1968, A's manager Bob Kennedy put Reggie in right field. "He has all the God-given gifts, all the tools," Kennedy said.

One of the A's coaches was Joe DiMaggio, the great New York Yankee center fielder. DiMaggio worked with Reggie. He gave Reggie tips on hitting, throwing, fielding, and base running. Coach DiMaggio was impressed with Reggie's talent and desire to learn. "He has made tremendous improvement, more than I ever imagined he could so quickly," DiMaggio said. "He'll strike out a lot, but he'll hit a lot of homers. I've seen him hit a ball 420 or 430 feet, so I know it's there."

Before the 1968 season began, the A's moved from Kansas City to Oakland, California. The Oakland fans quickly learned to watch Reggie. They never knew what to expect of him. Some games he would hit two home runs. Other games he would strike out four times. He would make spectacular catches. Or he would get hit on the head by a fly ball. He had a temper. Once he was so angry that he slammed his bat down and broke it. He hit 29 home runs as a rookie, but batted only .250 and struck out 171 times.

Slowly, Reggie settled down. He began to field better. He refused to let every strikeout bother him. "Sure, I strike out a lot," he said. "You don't have a chance if you don't swing. A lot of guys will strike out only 10 times a year. But how many home runs will they hit?"

In July 1968 Reggie married Juanita Campos, a girl he met at college. They were divorced five years later.

After the 1968 season, Reggie asked for a big raise. Charlie Finley, the A's owner, thought Reggie wanted too much money. Reggie angrily threatened to quit. "I don't have to play baseball for a living," he said. "There are other things I can do."

Finley finally gave Reggie a raise, though not as much as Reggie wanted. When the 1969 season began, the pitchers hardly could get Reggie out. He began to hit home runs at a record pace. By mid-season he hit 37 home runs. It seemed he might hit 75. The record was 61, set by Roger

Reggie socks a two-run homer against the New York Mets in 1973 World Series.

Maris in 1961. Before Maris, Babe Ruth had held the record, with 60 in 1927.

The fans cheered Reggie's hitting. Thousands came to ballparks all over the American League to see him. Newspaper and magazine writers, radio and television reporters wanted to talk to Reggie. "I ate it up," he said. "I enjoyed being the center of attention. Sometimes I get tired of it. But most of the time I need attention. I like to be admired."

One of Reggie's greatest days at bat came on June 15, 1969, at Boston's Fenway Park against the Red Sox. Reggie hit two home runs, two doubles, and a single in six times at bat, and drove in 10 runs in one game. "When you're hot nothing can stop you," Reggie said. "Everything keeps breaking your way. That day was my greatest in sports until I played in a World Series."

No hitter, not even one as good as Reggie, stays "hot." After the 1969 All-Star Game in July, Reggie went into a slump. He hit only 10 home runs the rest of the season. But he finished with 47 home runs, batted .275, and drove in 118 runs. His hitting helped the A's move up to second place after finishing sixth the year before.

Reggie now was a star. He asked for an even bigger raise than the year before. Finley offered him a raise, but not as much as Reggie wanted. Reggie held out. Spring training of 1970 was almost over when he finally gave in. The season started, but Reggie had not had enough practice. He struck out more often than ever and hit poorly.

Finley ordered A's manager John McNamara to bench Reggie. He even threatened to send him to the minor leagues. Reggie was angry and hurt. He felt sorry for himself. He sulked. Later Reggie said, "This experience made me a better man. It humbled me. I got too high and got taken down."

Finley finally let McNamara put Reggie back in the lineup. He started to hit well. But he finished the 1970 season with a batting average of only .237, with 23 home runs and 66 runs batted in.

Reggie never forgave Finley for benching him. But he decided to work as hard as he could to become a better ballplayer. He wanted to play well all the time.

Reggie started the 1971 season determined to do his best and let nothing bother him. The A's new manager, Dick Williams, liked Reggie. "He's a leader," Williams said. "The other guys respect him and follow him. He never stops hustling out there. He always has time to help out the other guys."

Reggie played steadily all season. He batted .277, hit 32 home runs, and drove in 80 runs. With Reggie leading the way, the A's won the division title in the American League West. They lost the playoffs to the Baltimore Orioles, though Reggie hit two home runs in the three games. Reggie was disappointed at not winning the American League pennant. After the last game he lay down on the dugout steps and cried. "We just weren't ready, I guess," he said.

Reggie and the A's were ready to win it all in 1972. Finley dressed them in gaudy green and gold uniforms. He had all the players grow mustaches. The A's looked like an old-time team. They were so colorful that fans all over the country turned out to see them play.

They also were good. They led the American League West from the first week of the season

Reggie waits in bus for trip to downtown Baltimore after arrival at airport for American League playoffs in October, 1974.

and won the division championship. Reggie did his share. He batted .265, with 25 home runs and 75 runs batted in. The A's played the Detroit Tigers in the playoffs. Each team won two of the first four games. The fifth game was to decide the American League championship.

In the second inning Reggie walked. He stole second base, then went to third on an out. Tiger pitcher Woody Fryman hit the next batter with a pitch. With runners on first and third, Reggie decided to try to steal home. About 30 feet from the plate, Reggie felt a great pain in his left leg. But he kept running. He safely slid under catcher Bill Freehan's tag at the plate to steal home. "I pulled a muscle," Reggie explained. "If I stopped I'd be out. If I kept going I'd tear up my leg. We needed the run so I kept going. But I was safe, and

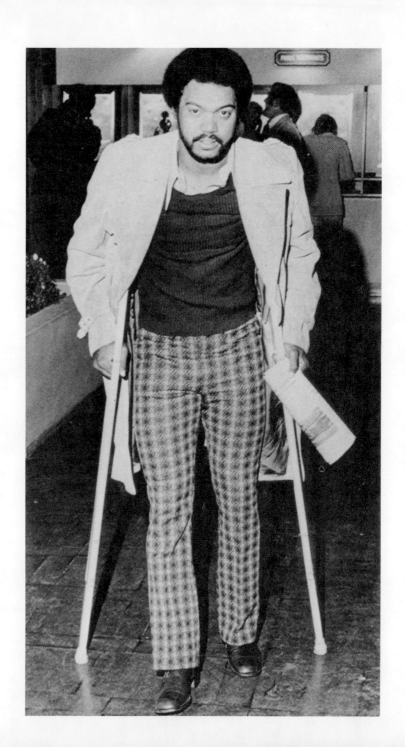

we went on to win the game, 2-1, and the American League pennant."

Reggie's leg was badly injured. Surgery was needed. He could not play for the A's in the World Series against the Cincinnati Reds. Without him, the A's won, four games to three. Reggie was happy for his team. But he was sad, too. He had not been part of the A's becoming the World Champions.

He decided that the 1973 season would be his "year." And it was. The A's won everything. Reggie was chosen the Most Valuable Player of the American League. He batted .293, his highest average as an Athletic, and led the league in home runs with 32 and runs batted in with 117.

Not everything went smoothly, though. The A's were rough. The players sometimes fought one

Reggie Jackson is shown at a press conference to announce the nominees for the Gillette Cavalcade of Champions awards in September, 1974.

another. Reggie had a fight with outfielder Bill North. He was ashamed of it. "After that (the fight), I looked back and said to myself, 'Shut up and play hard.' " At the end of the season, Reggie caught the flu. He was still weak when the play-offs against the Orioles opened. He was not much help. Still, the A's beat the Orioles and won the American League pennant.

Reggie was well by the time the World Series against the Cincinnati Reds opened. He helped win the sixth game 3-2 with two doubles and a single. In the seventh game he hit a two-run home run and made two fine catches. The A's won 5-2. The A's were World Champions for the second straight year. Reggie was voted the Most Valuable player of the World Series. "I was thinking about last year," he said. "I was thinking about being hurt, about my leg. Now it's a dream come true. I feel like a little boy again."

In 1974 the A's won the American League pennant and the World Series again. Reggie batted .289, hit 29 home runs, and drove in 93 runs. He hit a home run in the World Series as the A's beat the Los Angeles Dodgers in five games.

Three straight World Series championships made the A's one of the great baseball teams of all time. Reggie was their brightest star. But though Reggie and his teammates did not know it at the time, the A's great days were over.

The A's were fighting not only among themselves but with owner Finley. Many of the players did not like Finley because he was not paying them as much as they felt they should get. They did not like the way he ran the team himself rather than letting the manager call the plays. They were upset when Finley let the A's best pitcher, Catfish Hunter, get away to the Yankees. Reggie argued with Finley. He wanted to be traded to another team.

In spite of all the arguments, the A's won their fifth straight division championship in 1975. Reggie had a good season. He batted only .253, but led the league in home runs with 36 and drove in 104 runs. But the Boston Red Sox beat the A's in the championship playoffs to win the American League pennant. The A's clearly were slipping.

Finley began to trade away some of his best players. Just before the 1976 season started, he traded Reggie to the Baltimore Orioles. Reggie was glad to leave. "It wasn't me any more," he said. "I was losing my enthusiasm for baseball. I was getting tired of all the hassles."

He played well for the Orioles. In 1976, he batted .277, hit 27 home runs, and drove in 91 runs. But he already was looking forward to playing for the Yankees. His contract with the Orioles was running out. The baseball rules had changed.

Reggie with New York Yankees spring training instructor, Mickey Mantle, in 1977.

Soon he would be free to make a deal for himself. "I want to play in New York," Reggie admitted. "If I played in New York, they'd name a candy bar after me."

Reggie was thinking of the Baby Ruth candy bar. But it really isn't named after Babe Ruth. It is named after Ruth Cleveland, the first baby ever born to a President of the United States in the White House.

After the 1976 season, Reggie got his wish. George Steinbrenner, one of the Yankee owners, signed him to a five-year, $2,900,000 contract. At that time, it was the most money ever paid a baseball player. The poor boy had become a millionaire.

A lot was expected in New York of Reggie for all that money. He got a lot of attention. He also got into many arguments. Yankee manager Billy

Martin was hard on him. Many of his new team-mates were jealous of Reggie. Every argument, little or big, was spread all over the newspapers, and talked about on radio and television.

At the start of the 1977 season the Yankees did not play well. Reggie did not hit well. The fans booed him. They expected Reggie to play well because he had been paid so much money. In early August the Yankees were in third place, behind the Red Sox and the Orioles. Reggie was benched by Martin. They almost had a fight.

Owner Steinbrenner finally ordered Martin to put Reggie back in the lineup and to bat him "cleanup." During the next seven weeks the Yankees won 40 of 50 games. Reggie hit 13 home runs and drove in 49 runs as the Yankees rolled to the American League East division title. Oriole manager Earl Weaver said, "Reggie is the best

September player I've ever seen." Reggie finished the season with a batting average of .286, hit 32 home runs, and batted in 110 runs.

The Yankees went on to win the American League pennant by beating the Kansas City Royals in the championship playoffs. Reggie did not hit well in that series. Martin even benched him for the final game.

Then came the World Series against the Dodgers. Reggie hit a home run in the fourth game. He hit another one in the fifth game. Then came the sixth game. In one game Reggie outdid everyone before him, even the great Ruth, by slamming three home runs in a row. After the game, Reggie thought about his 1977 season. He thought about the arguments with Martin. He thought about the tremendous pressure on him to play well because of his high salary. "I wouldn't wish it on anybody,

what I went through," he said. "But it strength-
ened my character and humbled my personality."
Then he added, "You know . . . I want . . . people
to think of me as quite a person. On my tombstone
I would like 'He was respected and liked.' Like
me if you want to. But first respect me."

Most people respect Reggie because he is a
great baseball player. Some people respect Reggie
because he has a successful real estate business
in Arizona. Others like Reggie because he is
warm, outgoing, and generous. He gives money to
charity. He works with underprivileged young-
sters. He helps his friends. "If you've got money,
spread it around," Reggie says.

Most of all, people respect Reggie because they
know that whatever he does he wants to do it the
best. They know that he can get the "big" hits
when they are needed. He proved that again in the
1977 World Series.

Reggie continued to prove his greatness as a player in 1978. He again led the Yankees to an American League pennant and a World Series victory over the Dodgers.

As in 1977, Reggie was the center of attention because of his disputes with Martin. In mid-July, with the Yankees 14 games behind the Boston Red Sox, Martin suspended Reggie for five games because he failed to obey orders.

When owner Steinbrenner seemed to side with Reggie, Martin resigned as manager. The new manager was Bob Lemon, whom Reggie liked. "Bob Lemon is easier to play for," Reggie said. "If you can't play for him, you can't play for anyone."

The Yankees won 47 of their last 67 games under Lemon. Reggie hit as well in the last two months of the 1978 season as he had in 1977. The Yankees ended the regular season in a first place tie with Boston. In a playoff game for the Eastern

Division championship, Reggie hit a home run that gave the Yankees the margin for a 5-4 victory.

Reggie also helped defeat the Royals in the championship playoffs. He had six hits in the four games, and hit two home runs as he drove in six runs to lead the Yankees to another American League pennant.

Reggie played well in the World Series against the Dodgers, which the Yankees won in six games. He batted .391 and hit two home runs as he drove in eight runs. As in 1977, Reggie again was hailed as one of the great "September" players of all time.

Someone once asked Reggie what would have happened if he had taken up his father's trade of tailoring. "I would have been a super tailor, just like my Dad," Reggie answered.

He probably would have. Reggie has a driving need to succeed, to excel, to be noticed.

He even achieved his wish to have a candy bar named after him. "REGGIE" candy bars are sold.

JACKSON, Reginald Martinez (Reggie)

Year	Club	AVG.	G	AB	R	H	2B	3B	HR	RBI	BB	SO	SB
1966	Lewiston	.292	12	48	14	14	3	2	2	11	9	10	1
	Modesto	.299	56	221	50	66	6	0	21	50	15	71	3
1967	Birmingham	.293	114	413	84	121	26	17	17	58	44	87	17
	Kansas City	.178	35	118	13	21	4	4	1	6	10	46	1
1968	Oakland	.250	154	553	82	138	13	6	29	74	50	171	14
1969	Oakland	.275	152	549	123	151	36	3	47	118	114	142	13
1970	Oakland	.237	149	426	57	101	21	2	23	66	75	135	26
1971	Oakland	.277	150	567	87	157	29	3	32	80	63	161	16
1972	Oakland	.265	135	499	72	132	25	2	25	75	59	125	9
1973	Oakland	.293	151	539	99	158	28	2	32	117	76	111	22
1974	Oakland	.286	148	506	90	146	25	1	29	93	86	105	25
1975	Oakland	.253	157	593	91	150	39	3	36	104	67	133	17
1976	Baltimore	.277	134	498	84	138	27	2	27	91	54	108	28
1977	New York	.286	146	525	93	150	39	2	32	110	75	129	17
1978	New York	.274	139	511	82	140	13	5	27	97	58	133	14
M.L. Totals		.269	1650	5884	933	1582	299	35	340	1031	787	1499	212

Championship Series Records

Year	Club	AVG.	G	AB	R	H	2B	3B	HR	RBI	BB	SO	SB
1971	Oakland	.333	3	12	2	4	1	0	2	2	0	1	0
1972	Oakland	.278	5	18	1	5	1	0	0	2	1	6	2
1973	Oakland	.143	5	21	0	3	0	0	0	0	0	6	0
1974	Oakland	.167	4	12	0	2	1	0	0	1	5	2	0
1975	Oakland	.417	3	12	1	5	0	0	1	3	0	2	0
1977	New York	.125	5	16	1	2	0	0	0	1	2	2	1
1978	New York	.462	4	13	5	6	1	0	2	6	3	4	0
L.S.C. Totals		.260	29	104	10	27	4	0	5	15	11	23	3

World Series Record

Year	Club	AVG.	G	AB	R	H	2B	3B	HR	RBI	BB	SO	SB
1972	Oakland	(Eligible, replaced due to injury)											
1973	Oakland	.310	7	29	3	9	3	1	1	6	2	7	0
1974	Oakland	.286	5	14	3	4	1	0	1	1	5	3	1
1977	New York	.450	6	20	10	9	1	0	5	8	3	4	0
1978	New York	.391	6	23	2	9	1	0	2	8	3	7	0
W.S. Totals		.360	24	86	18	31	6	1	9	23	13	21	1

All-Star Game Record

Year	Club	AVG.	G	AB	R	H	2B	3B	HR	RBI	BB	SO	SB
1969	American	.000	1	2	0	0	0	0	0	0	1	0	0
1971	American	1.000	1	1	1	1	0	0	1	2	0	0	0
1972	American	.500	1	4	0	2	1	0	0	0	0	1	0
1973	American	.250	1	4	1	1	1	0	0	0	0	1	0
1974	American	.000	1	3	0	0	0	0	0	0	1	1	0
1975	American	.333	1	3	0	1	0	0	0	0	0	2	0
1977	American	.500	1	2	0	1	0	0	0	0	0	1	0
A.S. Totals		.316	7	19	2	6	2	0	1	2	2	6	0